P9-DYY-242

PLANTS
AND
FLOWERS

JOYCE POPE

Illustrated by
STUART PANTREY

Troll Associates

Nature Club Notes

Though you may not know it, you are a member of a special club called the Nature Club. To be a member you just have to be interested in living things and want to know more about them.

Members of the Nature Club respect all living things. They look at and observe plants and animals, but do not collect or kill them. If you take a magnifying glass or a bug box with you when you go out, you will be able to see the details of even tiny plants, animals, or fossils. Also, you should always take a notebook and pencil so that you can make a drawing of anything you don't know. Don't say "But I can't draw" – even a simple sketch can help you identify your discovery later on. There are many books that can help you name the specimens you have found and tell you something about them.

Your bag should also contain a waterproof jacket and something to eat. It is silly to get cold, wet, or hungry when you go out. Always tell your parents or a responsible adult where you are going and what time you are coming back.

Leave flowers for other people to enjoy. Remember, that they are the food for many sorts of animals. If you pick them, small creatures such as bees and other insects may starve, and the birds and mammals that depend on them or the seeds that they would make may also go hungry.

Never, never, dig up wild plants. In many parts of the world it is illegal, and in some places, picking wild flowers is forbidden.

Library of Congress Cataloging-in-Publication Data

Pope, Joyce.
    Plants and flowers / by Joyce Pope ; illustrated by Stuart Pantrey.
        p.   cm. — (Nature club)
    Includes index.
    Summary: Discusses how plants live, develop, and reproduce and examines such natural variations as plants without flowers and flesh-eating plants.
    ISBN 0-8167-2779-1 (lib. bdg.)   ISBN 0-8167-2780-5 (pbk.)
    1. Botany—Juvenile literature. [1. Botany.   2. Plants.]
I. Pantrey, Stuart, ill.   II. Title.   III. Series.
QK49.P66   1994
581—dc20   91-45378

Published by Troll Associates

Copyright © 1994 by Eagle Books

All rights reserved. No part of this book may be reproduced or utilized in any form or by any means, electronic or mechanical, including photocopying, recording or by any storage and retrieval system, without permission in writing from the Publisher.

Designed by Cooper Wilson, London
Edited by Kate Woodhouse
Printed in the U.S.A.
10 9 8 7 6 5 4 3 2 1

Contents

Introduction

Plants are found almost everywhere there is light, warmth, and some water. There are plants on land, in the sea, and in rivers. There are even plants in deserts. Huge trees, orchids, grasses, mosses, and tiny algae are all plants. They look so different from one another that you might wonder – what makes a plant a plant?

Plants are different from animals in two important ways. They cannot move about and they are generally able to make their own food. The process by which plants make food is called *photosynthesis*. Plants use energy from the sun as fuel for this process. The sun's energy is trapped by the green substance in leaves called *chlorophyl*. Plants take in a gas called *carbon dioxide* from the air and combine it with water and minerals from the soil to make food. They give off oxygen, which animals need to breathe.

◄ Although plants are the largest and oldest living things on Earth, some like these diatoms, are so small that you need a microscope to see them. These tiny plants can move about almost like animals.

▲ Sequoia, or "redwood" trees, found only in the Western United States, are the largest of all living things.

4

Plants are also the basic food producers for animals. Even meat-eating animals such as lions need plants to survive.

There are a few kinds of plants that cannot make their own food. They are able to grow on other organisms and get the food they need from them.

◄ Many creatures, such as antelopes or rabbits, feed only on plants. Other animals, like cheetahs, must also eat plants, but they get them second-hand through the flesh of herbivores.

How Plants Live

Almost all plants need light to live. They cannot survive in caves or the deep sea where the sun never reaches. Only fungi can live without light. Plants spread their branches, and leaves stretch upward and outward to catch as much light as possible.

Most plants, like animals, are made up of a huge number of tiny cells. Each plant cell has a stiff wall. Some cells are very long and thin and carry water from one part of the plant to another. Others carry food to be stored or used for growth.

The plants we know best, such as trees and garden plants, are divided into several parts. Their roots anchor them in the ground and take up water and minerals from the earth.

▶ When you dig up a plant you can see its roots. Roots anchor the plant in soil. They collect water and food, and sometimes they also store them. The stems support the leaves, flowers, and fruit.

▼ It is easy to see how plants need light. Under the shady leaves of trees such as beeches or firs, hardly anything can grow. Outside the wood where there is more light, the ground is covered with small plants.

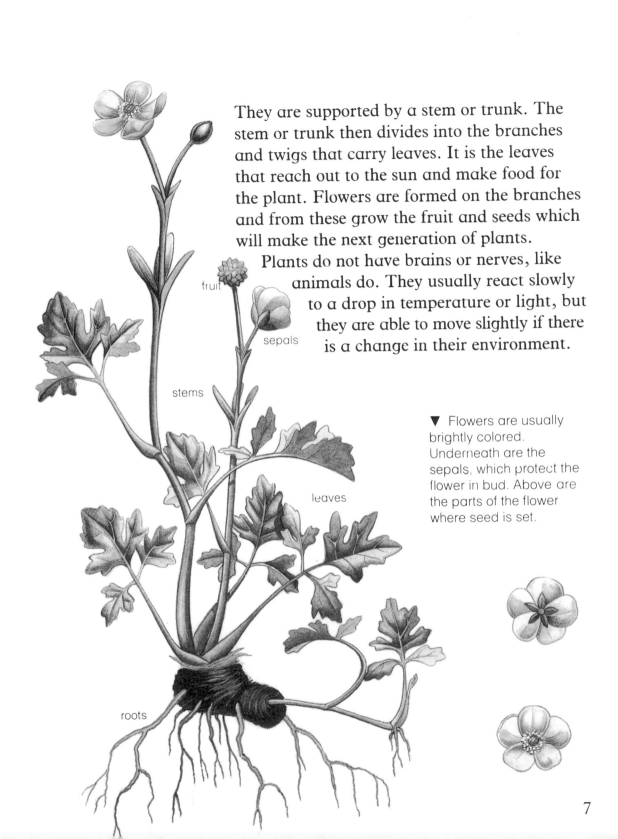

They are supported by a stem or trunk. The stem or trunk then divides into the branches and twigs that carry leaves. It is the leaves that reach out to the sun and make food for the plant. Flowers are formed on the branches and from these grow the fruit and seeds which will make the next generation of plants.

Plants do not have brains or nerves, like animals do. They usually react slowly to a drop in temperature or light, but they are able to move slightly if there is a change in their environment.

fruit

sepals

stems

leaves

▼ Flowers are usually brightly colored. Underneath are the sepals, which protect the flower in bud. Above are the parts of the flower where seed is set.

roots

What Is a Flower?

Flowers are beautiful. We enjoy their bright colors and their smell. We grow them because they give us pleasure. To many small creatures, flowers give shelter and food. Their *petals* are landing strips, and the *nectar* and *pollen* they produce is good to eat. But to a plant, flowers are the way of making certain that there will be another generation of plants.

Flowers contain male and female parts. The main female part is called the *pistil*. It contains the *ovary* and its *ovules*, which are unfertilized seeds. The male parts are called *stamens*, which produce pollen. Grains of pollen must reach the ovules to make seeds that can grow. The ovary and stamens are surrounded and protected by petals and *sepals*.

▼ This picture is a cross-section of a flower. The sepals and petals are arranged around the stem, with the female parts, the stigma, *style* and ovary, in the center. The male parts, or stamens, are on either side of the *stigma*. Most flowers have both male and female parts. A few kinds of plants have flowers with either stamens or ovaries, but not both.

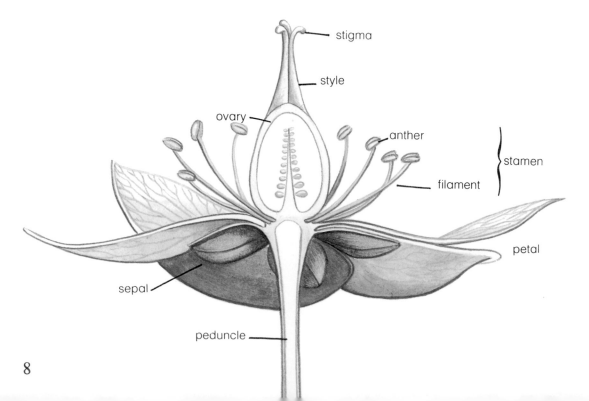

8

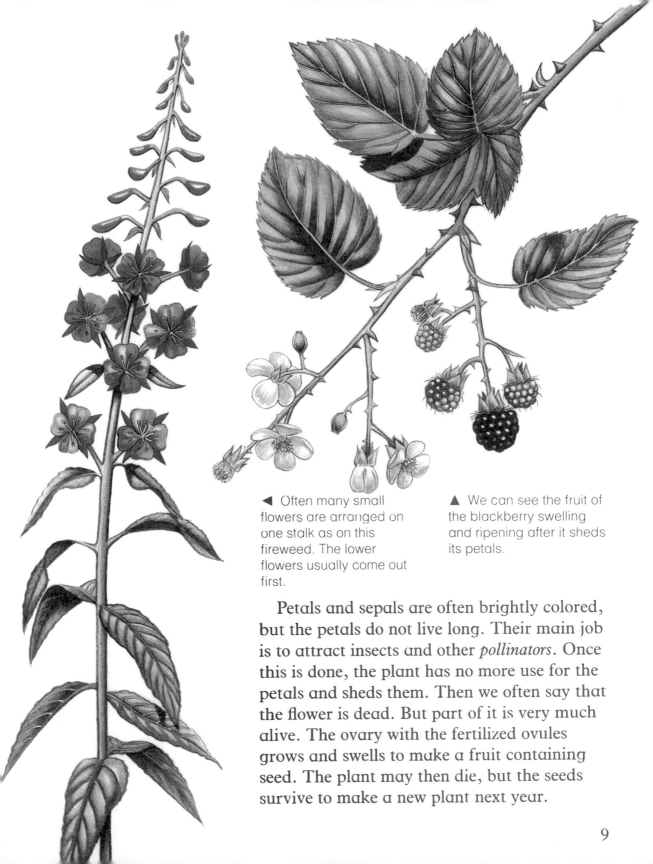

◄ Often many small flowers are arranged on one stalk as on this fireweed. The lower flowers usually come out first.

▲ We can see the fruit of the blackberry swelling and ripening after it sheds its petals.

Petals and sepals are often brightly colored, but the petals do not live long. Their main job is to attract insects and other *pollinators*. Once this is done, the plant has no more use for the petals and sheds them. Then we often say that the flower is dead. But part of it is very much alive. The ovary with the fertilized ovules grows and swells to make a fruit containing seed. The plant may then die, but the seeds survive to make a new plant next year.

Pollination

During pollination, pollen grains are taken from the stamen, the male part of the flower, and put onto a long outgrowth of the ovary called the *style*. The top of the style is known as the *stigma*. It is usually knobbed or cross-shaped and is sticky, so any pollen that touches it is held there.

Each pollen grain is tiny, far too small to see without a microscope. When pollen is on the stigma, it starts to grow. It pushes a long tube down the style and into the ovary. In the ovary, the pollen tube fuses with one of the ovules.

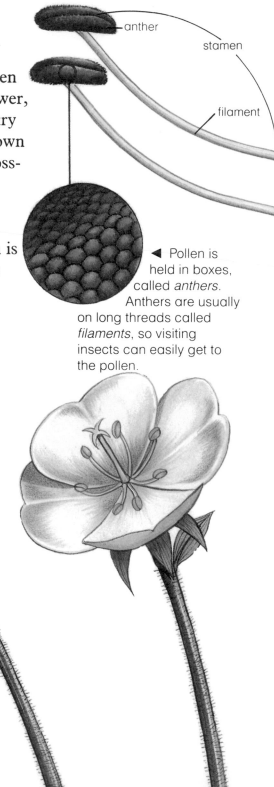

anther

stamen

filament

◄ Pollen is held in boxes, called *anthers*. Anthers are usually on long threads called *filaments*, so visiting insects can easily get to the pollen.

► Most flowers open for only a few days. A few, like evening primroses, open at sunset, to be pollinated by night-flying insects. By morning only the ovary, with its fertilized ovules, remains.

This is *pollination*. The ovule can then grow into a seed. It may be months before the seed is ripe. During this time it is protected and fed by the plant. Very few of the seeds will form new plants, but each plant makes so many seeds that there are plenty to spare.

If the pollen of a buttercup landed on the stigma of a hollyhock, there would be no pollination, as pollen must go to another plant of the same kind. If the pollen from the stamen lands on its own stigma, fewer seeds set. This does not often happen, as a plant's pollen is usually ripe at a different time from the few days when the stigma is ready to take it.

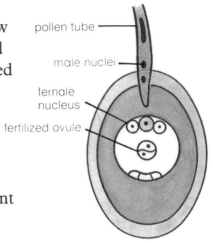

pollen tube

male nuclei

female nucleus

fertilized ovule

▲ This diagram shows the tube, growing from a pollen grain, about to enter an ovule in a plant's ovary. The tube carries male nuclei, which fuse with a female nucleus.

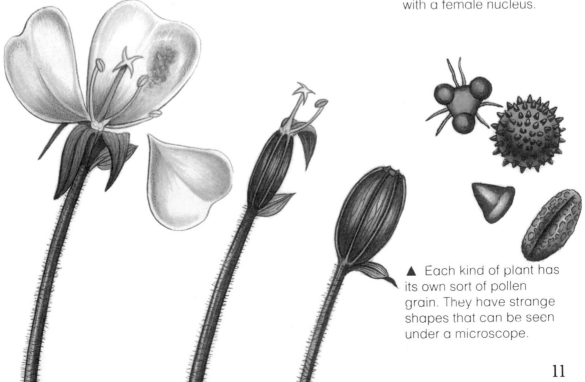

▲ Each kind of plant has its own sort of pollen grain. They have strange shapes that can be seen under a microscope.

Flowers and Insects

The first flowers protected their delicate stamens with leaves that grew around them. Flying insects must have found this a good place to rest, to shelter from the wind and enemies. If the stamens were ripe and producing pollen, the flowers were even more attractive, as pollen is a good food for insects. Some of this pollen stuck to the insects' bodies and was carried to the next flower the insects visited.

Other animals such as spiders sometimes got into flowers, but they were not very good pollinators. Insects could fly from one bloom to another very quickly and easily. Plants have changed in many ways through the ages, so the right insects are attracted to their flowers.

fragrant orchid

yellow archangel

marsh violet

birdsfoot trefoil

white clover

evening primrose

foxglove

The protective leaves which we call petals are brightly colored. Insects can see them easily among green leaves. Most petals are broad so insects can land on them. Many wild flowers have thin stems that sway in the wind and this helps to attract the insects' attention. Some flowers are star-shaped, which also makes them easy to see. Other flowers have a strong scent, and many produce a sugary substance called nectar. Insects visit flowers to collect nectar or pollen as food.

▲ Many flowers change color toward the center of the petals. Patches or lines of a color deeper than the main shade of the petal draw an insect toward the place where it will find pollen and nectar.

► Many insects visit flowers to find food, or sometimes to rest. There are even some bees called "Flower Sleepers" because they rest and sleep in the protection of a flower's petals.

Development of Insects

The first insects probably fed on dead plants and animals. Some of their descendants still do, but others began to feed on living plants. The insects that are most important to plants today did not develop until much later, when flowering plants began. These insects, which include beetles, butterflies, moths, bees, and flies are different from the ancient species. Their lives are divided into several stages. The first stage is the egg. A *grub* or *caterpillar* hatches from the egg. The grub looks nothing like its parents and it cannot fly. It just feeds and grows until it changes into a *pupa* or *chrysalis*. Finally an adult insect, which can fly, emerges from the chrysalis.

Adult insects do not grow, but most require food so they can fly to search for mates. Plant nectar is the perfect food, as it can be changed quickly into energy. Insects that search for nectar are the plants' main pollinators. They often have hairy bodies to which the pollen sticks easily. They have large eyes which can see bright colors. Many of them have long tongues which reach nectar deeply hidden in the flower. In some cases, particular insects have developed a partnership with certain flowers and are their only pollinators.

▲ Bees find flowers by color and scent. A foraging bee collects nectar with its tongue.

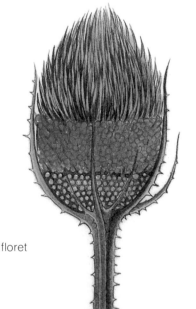

▶ It is easy to see bees or butterflies, but tiny insects are also important pollinators. Small beetles may shelter in a teasel flower, carrying pollen from one floret to another.

floret

14

antennae

eye

butterfly's head

tongue

▲▶ Butterflies and moths have even longer tongues than bees. They suck nectar from deep in the tubes of flowers where bees cannot reach.

tongue

Bird- and Bat-Pollinated Flowers

Some plants have flowers that are pollinated by birds or tropical bats. These creatures have the same advantages for plants that flying insects do, as they can fly directly from one flower to another carrying pollen on their feathers or fur. Most bird and bat flowers are large and strongly built. The pollinating birds and bats are quite small, but they are much bigger than most insects. The flowers usually have the ovaries below the level of the petals. This means that the beaks and claws of the pollinators will not damage the ovaries, although the petals may be badly torn.

▶ Hummingbirds can hover in front of a flower while they are feeding from it. As they drink the nectar, pollen sticks to their beaks and tongues. They carry the pollen to the next flower they visit.

▼ Most hummingbirds have long beaks. Their tongue is trough-shaped, so nectar can flow along it. The tip is like a brush, good for collecting pollen and insects in the flower.

cross-section of a hummingbird's tongue

Many insects cannot see pure red – they see it as black. Birds can see red well, so bird-pollinated plants are often bright red. They produce a great deal of nectar, but it is more watery than nectar found in insect-pollinated plants. Hummingbirds, sunbirds, small parrots, and honeyeaters are all pollinators. They probably also feed on insects that they catch inside the flowers.

Bat-pollinated flowers usually open at night. They are often pale green or purplish and have a powerful, musty scent. Many of these plants are pollinated by only one type of bat.

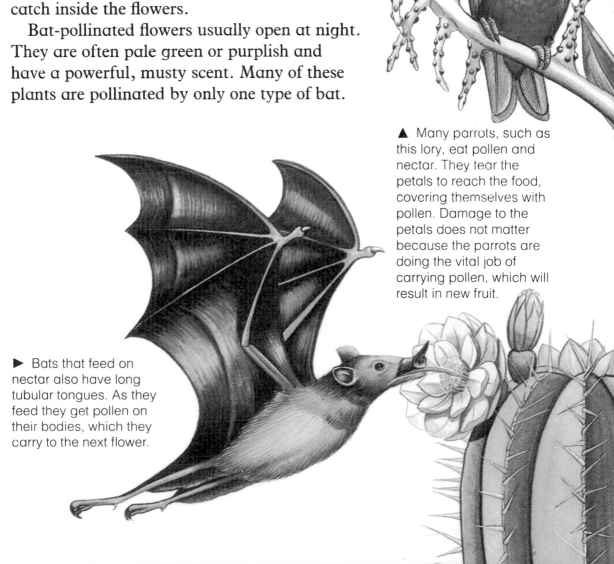

▲ Many parrots, such as this lory, eat pollen and nectar. They tear the petals to reach the food, covering themselves with pollen. Damage to the petals does not matter because the parrots are doing the vital job of carrying pollen, which will result in new fruit.

▶ Bats that feed on nectar also have long tubular tongues. As they feed they get pollen on their bodies, which they carry to the next flower.

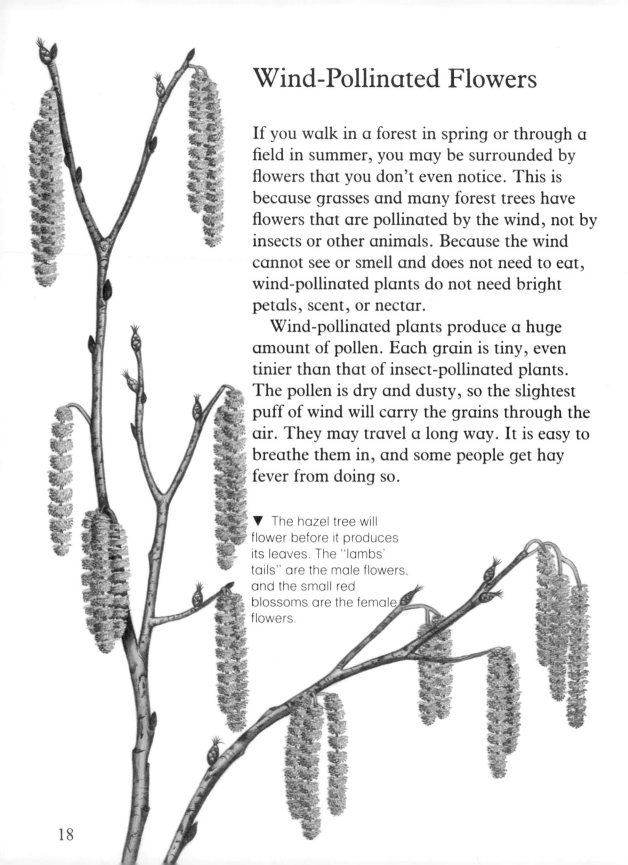

Wind-Pollinated Flowers

If you walk in a forest in spring or through a field in summer, you may be surrounded by flowers that you don't even notice. This is because grasses and many forest trees have flowers that are pollinated by the wind, not by insects or other animals. Because the wind cannot see or smell and does not need to eat, wind-pollinated plants do not need bright petals, scent, or nectar.

Wind-pollinated plants produce a huge amount of pollen. Each grain is tiny, even tinier than that of insect-pollinated plants. The pollen is dry and dusty, so the slightest puff of wind will carry the grains through the air. They may travel a long way. It is easy to breathe them in, and some people get hay fever from doing so.

▼ The hazel tree will flower before it produces its leaves. The "lambs' tails" are the male flowers, and the small red blossoms are the female flowers.

◀ After pollination from the catkins, part of the female flowers grow to form acorns – the oak tree's fruit.

The flowers of wind-pollinated deciduous trees are often tassle-like *catkins*. They appear each spring, before the leaves appear. With no leaves to block the wind, the pollen is easily blown about. Grasses have their flowers on long stems above the level of grass leaves in the field. Trees often have separate male and female flowers, the females are usually only tiny bunches of red stigmas. Next time you see an oak tree with catkins, look for the female flowers. Although they are small, they will produce the crop of acorns. Coniferous trees are also wind-pollinated. Their flowers look like tiny cones.

quaking grass

sweet vernal

Timothy grass

perennial rye grass

stigma

stamen

stamen

stigma

stigma

stamen

Seeds

Most seeds develop quickly. Some take only a month, though some pine seeds need three years to mature. As the seeds grow inside the ovary, the outer walls of the ovary change. They often swell and become soft and brightly colored to form a fruit. The colors and sweet scent attract animals that are hungry. Some of the seeds are destroyed, but there are always enough for the next generation. Often only the sweet part is eaten, and the seeds are left, as happens when we eat an apple.

When the seeds of a flowering plant are ripe, they must be taken away from the parent plant. If they were to drop to the ground near their parents, the area would be crowded and the plants would not flourish. Some plants have sticky burs that hold their seeds. The burs catch on an animal's fur and are dropped in a new area away from the parent plant. So once again, flowering plants depend on animals or the wind, as they cannot move.

▼ Fruits that fall to the ground, like beech nuts, may be eaten or stored by a bird or a squirrel. Often an animal that buries a fruit or seed does not return to eat it. The seed may then germinate and grow. It soon produces two special leaves, which make its first food. The main shoot of the young tree, with normal leaves, develops above this.

◄ When the fruit of a beech tree is ripe, the husk dries and splits and the fruit falls to the ground.

▶ The tuft of hairs attached to the seed of plants such as the creeping thistle is called its parachute.

When you see a bird gobbling berries, you might think that no seeds could survive. In fact, the seeds in berries are usually designed to be eaten. They pass through the bird's digestive system unharmed. The seed's tough outer coat may be weakened by stomach acids, and this will help the seed to germinate.

Many other plants have seeds that grow tufts of hair. When they are ripe, they are lifted by warm currents of air and carried away by the wind. They may travel across half a continent before they drop back to the ground. Many plants on remote islands, such as Hawaii, grew from plumed seeds that were originally carried across the sea by the wind.

creeping thistle

oak leaves and acorns

Plants Without Flowers

Seaweeds, mosses, and ferns are plants that never have flowers. Most of them live in moist and shady places, which is why you often find ferns in woodlands. Plants without flowers are usually small, although some seaweeds called kelp may be over 100 feet (about 30 m) long. In prehistoric times, some plants without flowers grew to be as large as gigantic trees.

Plants without flowers do not form seeds. Long ago people were puzzled by this and thought the seeds must be invisible. They believed that if you found bracken seeds *you* would become invisible. We now know that ferns and other flowerless plants are formed in various ways, usually by *spores*. In land plants, these are dust-fine particles that may grow on the *fronds* or develop in special capsules.

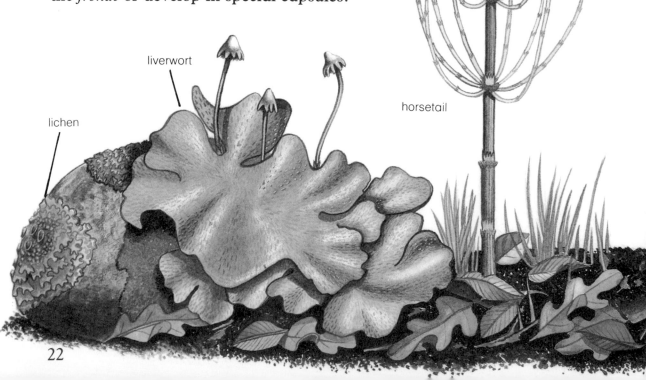

liverwort

lichen

horsetail

The spores are carried by the wind, and if they fall on suitable ground, they germinate and grow. At first, they look nothing like the parent plant. They make a plant on which male and female organs grow. The male produces tiny, active, animal-like organisms that swim through a film of water and join with the female cells. New spore-forming plants are produced from this.

▼ Spores develop on the back of the fronds of many kinds of ferns.

fern

fly agaric fungus

sulphur tuft fungus

moss

Flesh-Eating Plants

Some plants live in places where their roots can find very little food. In order to survive, they use their leaves to trap and digest small animals. The largest animal that a flesh-eating plant can trap is a mouse, but most can catch only insects.

Flesh-eating plants take good care not to trap the insects that might pollinate their flowers. The traps are always formed by the leaves. The flowers have very long stems, so it is unlikely that an insect will be caught accidentally as it hunts for nectar and pollen.

bladderwort

butterwort

sundew

The traps made by the leaves are like the traps that humans have invented to catch animals. Sundews and butterworts use sticky traps, like flypaper. The two main sorts of pitcher plants use pitfall traps into which insects slide and cannot escape. The Venus's-flytrap uses its leaves to make a spring trap. Underwater, bladderworts make vacuum traps, which suck in small creatures. Tiny flesh-eating fungi in the soil make their cells into a noose around the bodies of eelworms.

Once an insect is caught, the leaves produce a liquid like the digestive juices of animals. The prey is killed, and its body is broken down and absorbed through the surface of the leaf. The tough, indigestible bits are left and quickly blow away in the wind.

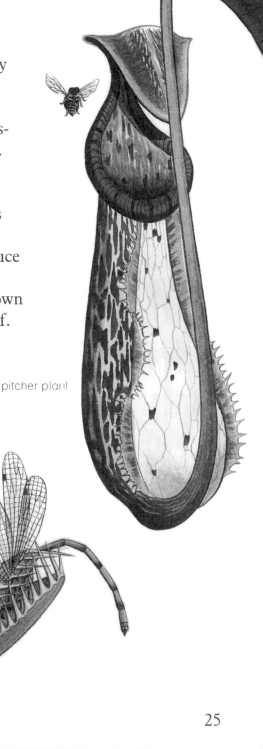

pitcher plant

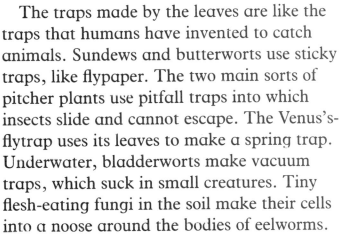

Venus's—fly trap catching a damsel fly

25

Orchids

There are more than 30,000 different sorts of orchids, most of which grow in the tropics. Orchid flowers are famous for their brilliant colors and strange shapes, but they all have six petals, like the flowers of tulips. One, called the *lip petal*, is much larger than the others. At the back of the lip petal there is often a tube containing nectar to feed pollinating insects.

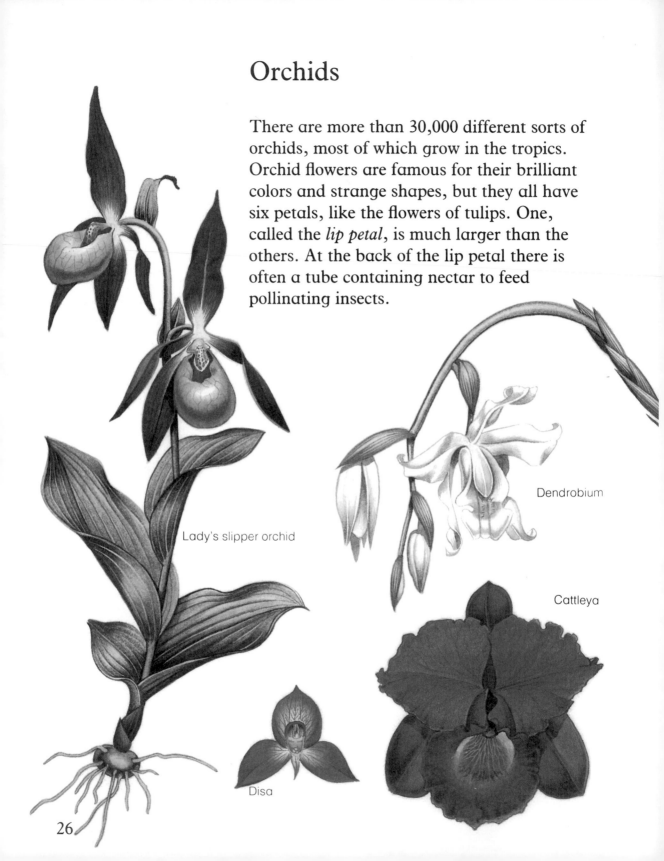

Lady's slipper orchid

Dendrobium

Cattleya

Disa

The pollen of almost all orchids is formed in clumps called *pollinia*. An insect is guided by the shape of the lip petal to the part of the flower where a pollinium is stuck to its body. When it visits the next orchid, some of the pollen is removed before another pollinium is added. Many orchids are pollinated by only one kind of insect. In some cases, the flower looks like a female insect and males try to mate with it. In other cases, the orchid looks like an enemy and the pollinators try to drive it away. Some South American orchids drug visiting bees so that they fall onto the pollinia.

Orchid seeds are smaller than those of any other plant. They are so tiny that there is hardly any room in them for food. The seedlings are partly fed by special fungi called *mycorrhiza*. Even so, it may take over fifteen years for an orchid plant to grow enough to make a flower, which is a very good reason for not picking wild orchids!

▼ This beetle has pollinia from three flowers stuck to its body. Some of the pollinia have broken slightly as the beetle brushed the pollen onto another flower.

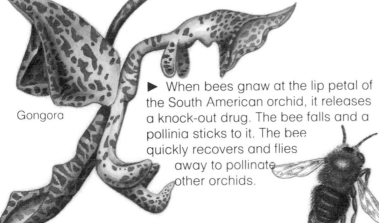

Gongora

▶ When bees gnaw at the lip petal of the South American orchid, it releases a knock-out drug. The bee falls and a pollinia sticks to it. The bee quickly recovers and flies away to pollinate other orchids.

bee orchid

27

Plants and People

People have used plants since prehistoric times. First they used plants as food, then as wood for fires, building shelters, and making weapons. Later, plant fibers were used for making ropes and for weaving baskets and clothes. Plant colors were used for dyes, the most famous of which is called *woad*. The strong chemicals in plants were used for flavoring and medicines. People have always enjoyed the beauty of flowers. The ancient Egyptians were among the first people to have elaborate gardens.

Today we still use plants in these and many other ways. Wood is used to make paper, houses, and furniture. The plants we eat grow in many parts of the world. Look along the shelves of your supermarket and see how many countries your fruit and vegetables have come from.

People have changed plants to make them produce more food. Wild grasses from the Middle East now provide wheat, barley, and oats. Another grass from India and China gives us rice, while corn comes from a Mexican grass. Plants have been altered by cultivation so they taste better. Our apples and plums are far better than their wild ancestors, for instance.

But most plants have not benefited from human attention. Forests have been cut down to take the choicest woods, while many plants have been destroyed through bad farming methods. Only now are we beginning to understand that we must conserve plants, for they give us so much that we cannot possibly replace if they die out.

Glossary

anther   the organ at the top of the filament that secretes and discharges pollen.

carbon dioxide   a gas that forms a small part of the earth's atmosphere. Much of it is made as a waste product of human and animal breathing. Plants combine the gas with water and minerals from the soil to make food.

caterpillar   the creature that hatches from the egg laid by a butterfly or a moth. Caterpillars do not look like their parents. They cannot fly and spend most of their lives feeding.

catkin   the kind of flower produced by many sorts of trees. Catkins are pollinated by the wind so they do not have petals or nectar or a strong smell. Many catkins are either male or female. The males produce large amounts of pollen, the females have stigmas and ovaries for producing seeds.

chlorophyl   a green substance found in the leaves and stems of plants. It enables them to use the power of the sunlight to make sugars and starches from carbon dioxide, water and minerals.

chrysalis   the non-feeding stage in which a caterpillar changes into a butterfly or a moth.

coniferous   cone-bearing trees.

deciduous   trees that lose their leaves at a certain time each year, and later grow new leaves.

filament   the long, slender thread of a stamen.

frond   the stem and leaves of a non-flowering plant, such as a fern.

grub   the young of an insect that does not look like its parent. Caterpillars are grubs, so are the young of bees, flies, and beetles, among many others.

lip petal   an enlarged petal on the lower side of some flowers, like those of the dead nettle, that do not have a regular shape. In orchids, the lip petal is often fantastically shaped and colored to attract insects.

mycorrhiza   small fungi that grow around the roots of many plants. It is not known exactly how they work, but the plants get some food from the fungi. In their early years, orchids could not survive without mycorrhiza.

nectar   a sugary solution made by flowers. It helps to attract and feed the flying creatures (insects, bats and birds) that pollinate the flowers.

ovary   the part of a female animal that produces eggs. In plants, it is the part at the base of the flower in which ovules are formed, and, after pollination, grows into seeds.

ovule   the part of a plant that grows into a seed after pollination.

petals   the brightly colored part of most flowers. Petals help to protect the delicate male and female parts of the plant and also attract pollinators.

photosynthesis the process by which plants build up food (sugars and starches) in their leaves or other green parts. To do this they use carbon dioxide from the atmosphere, water and minerals from the soil, and the Sun's energy.

pistil the part of the plant that contains the ovary and ovules.

pollen the male part of a plant. Pollen looks like tiny grains on the stamens. When these are carried to the stigma of another plant of the same kind, the pollen begins to grow. Part of it fuses with an ovule, which is then pollinated and becomes a seed.

pollinators animals (mainly insects, but also some bats, a few kinds of birds, and very few mammals) that carry pollen from one plant to another so that pollination may take place.

pollinia the special bundles of pollen that are part of many kinds of orchids.

pupa the inactive part of the life of many kinds of insects. During this time the animals' larval bodies break down and rebuild themselves in the adult shape.

sepals a ring of leaflike organs that surround the petals of a flower. They protect the flower when it is in bud but as it opens they are usually folded back.

spores the dust-fine part of a non-flowering plant that grows into a new plant, often one that does not look like the parent.

stamens the part of a flower that produces the pollen.

stigma the sticky top section of the female part of a flower. When pollen of the right kind lands on the stigma, it is held there and grows so that pollination takes place.

style in a flower, the column that supports the stigma so that it is in the best position to catch pollen brought to it by insects or other pollinators.

woad a plant related to cabbages and wallflowers found in much of Europe and the cooler parts of Asia. It has bright yellow flowers, but the leaves give a bright blue dye. Woad was used by ancient Britons to stain their skin, and later to dye clothes.

Index